Messages of Hope

Volume 1

Earline May

Earline May

Copyright©2023 Earline May

Messages of Hope is a compilation of messages I have written and preached over my many years as a Pastor. It is my prayer and heart's desire that they may be a source of Hope, strength and encouragement to you wherever you are in your life's journey.

Read each one carefully and prayerfully and allow God the Father to speak to you. May you see yourself as the special person that God sees you.

May you find renewed hope for living. May you find a good Church Home that you may worship in every Sunday. God wants to be with you, he wants you to be with Him.

May it be so in your life.

God Bless You!

Index

- Love the Ultimate Test 1
- Knowing the Mind of God 5
- Jehosophat the Overcomer 9
- Working for Christ on the job 12
- Reaching Out 15
- Delivered to Serve 19
- Channels of Grace 22
- A Life Sentence 25
- Religious or Christian 28
- Spiritual Diet 32
- Not I But Christ 35
- The Holy Spirit at work in our life 37
- The Two Sons 38
- Where do we go from here? 41
- The Great Commission 44
- Dare to be a Daniel 47
- Thomas Delivered from Doubt 51
- A Life of Obedience 54
- All You Could Hope For 58

MESSAGES OF HOPE

The messages within this book are an accumulation of over 50 years of ministry. I am a Retired Salvation Army Pastor who enjoys writing and reading.

Over the first 30+ years of my Pastoral Ministry I pastored over 20 Corps (Churches), from Upstate New York to the great state of Ohio.

Throughout my ministry I have seen the faithfulness of God at work in my life and in the life of my congregants.

God showed up each and every time to meet needs. His grace is always sufficient, His love has no limits, and His love is available to all.

He is a God that loves you, who wants you to love Him. He is the Protector, Provider, Strong Tower.

He is all of that, and so much more.

It is my prayer that as you read each of these messages, you will be encouraged in your journey. If you are unsaved, it is my prayer that you will seek and find Him before it is eternally too late. He is waiting, He is knocking at your heart's door, will you let Him in. He is coming again to take His Church to be with Him forever in His Kingdom. Will you be in that number?

G

Love the Ultimate Test
1 John 4:7-12

The best way to get along with people is to love them! It sounds easy, doesn't it? For many people it is a very difficult thing to do.

Webster defines love as: unselfish concern that freely accepts another in loyalty and seeks his good. Brotherly concern for others. Love! A very misunderstood word in the English language. Perhaps because it has so many meanings. Our Scripture today tells us of the pattern which God set down for us to follow. The eleventh verse says, "Beloved, if God so loved us, we ought also to love one another."

This is the ultimate test of not only Christians but sinners as well. Before a sinner can come to repentance, he must first love. Loving one another more by our actions and words and in everything we do should be the ultimate goal.

As we look at this word Love, we can see what we must do to reach the ultimate goal of perfect love. To pass the ultimate test of love and reach perfect love we must first realize:

Love is Displayed

God is Love. 1 John 4:16 says: "And we have known and believed the love that God has to us, God is Love. All love is from God. Unless we abide in love we cannot abide in God."

Illustration: A man was riding in the country and saw a weather vane. Inscribed on the weather vane were the words: God is Love. No matter what direction the wind blows the message is the same, God is still love.

For better relations with others. We must love one another. Treat others as you would want to be treated. The golden rule states: "Do unto others that you want done to you!"

Love must go beyond ourself. It must show in everything that we do.

I was Counselling a young couple who were planning to get married, counseled each individually and together. As I was counselling the young bride to be, I asked her if she loved the man she was soon to marry. She said, "Yes, I wash his clothes, I make his meals, I wash his car." I said to her, "I said to her, "I didn't ask you if you worked hard for him, I asked if you loved him." Will you love him when he is sick and his body so full of pain, and he may not be able to love you back? Will you love him when he wrecked the car because he made some careless mistake". That's the real test of love.

Love has been so beautifully defined in this manner:

"Love is giving with no thought of getting. It is tenderness enfolding with strength to protect. It is forgiveness without thought of the thing forgiven. It is understanding of human weakness with knowledge of the true man shining through.

It is quiet in the midst of turmoil. It is trust in God with no though of self. It is the one altogether lovely, the love in a mother's eyes, the glory of the sacrifice, the quiet assurance of protection.

It is the expectation of our Father's promise coming true. It is the refusal to see anything but good in our fellowman. It is the glory that comes with selflessness and the power that comes with the assurance of the Father's love for His children. It is the voice that says no to our brother, though yes might be more easily said. It is resistance to the world's lust and greed thus becoming a positive law of annihilation to error.

Love, one of the things we can give constantly and become increasingly rich in the giving. Love can take no offense, for it cannot know that which it cannot itself conceive. It cannot hurt or be hurt, for it is the purest reflection of God for good. It is the one eternal, indestructible force for good. It is the will of God, preparing, planning and proposing always what is best for all His universe.

There is no difficulty that enough love will not conquer. No disease that enough love cannot heal. No door that enough love cannot open. No gulf that enough love cannot bridge. No wall that enough love cannot tear down. No sin that enough love cannot redeem. It makes no difference how deeply seated may be the trouble you are in, how hopeless the outlook, how great the mistake, a sufficient realization of love will dissolve it all. If only you could love enough, you would be the happiest and most powerful being.

In 1965 Hal David wrote the words to a very popular song, "What the World Needs Now is Love."

What the world needs now, is love, sweet love
It's the only thing that there is just too little of
What the world needs now is love, sweet love.
No not just for some, but for everyone.

All these years later the world still needs love. The kind of love that will stand the test of time. The kind of love that will not fail.

Did you pass the Ultimate test of Love?

It is not us that must love but God loves us supremely. He loves us to the depths of hell. Corrie Ten Boom said, "There is no well so deep that enough Love cannot reach!" What a wonderful thought!

You can't be bad enough.

God showed us perfect love in John 3:16 which says, "For God so loved the world, (you and me) that He gave His only begotten Son (Jesus), that whosoever believes in Him should not perish but have everlasting life." God loves you so much, that He gave His Son to die on a cross for your sins. Jesus who was without sin, took on our sin." Oh, such love. Thank you, God, for loving me enough, that you would die for me.

Knowing the mind of God
Ecclesiastes 9: 16-17

How many times, as a child, were you asked the question: "What do you want to be when you grow up?" I am sure that our answers changed with our age- most five-year-old boys want to be a fireman, some want to be a teacher, others want to be doctors. It is fun to dream when you are children, but the question becomes more crucial as you approach your teen and adult years. What vocation do you want to pursue?

As Christians, we need to realize that God does have special plans for our life. It doesn't necessarily have to be full-time Christian service, but it may be. When I was thinking about my future as a teen, I wanted to be a nurse. Went to biology class, had to dissect a frog, fainted and quickly realized that nursing may not be a good fit for me. I tried one part time job after another trying to figure it out. It began for me a lifetime of ministry. That passage of Scripture is Jeremiah 29:11, "For I know the plans I have for you, declares the Lord, "plans to prosper you and not to harm you, plans to give you hope and a future."

We need to understand that God does not play games with us. His will for us is not some mysterious thing that He dangles just out of our reach. God does promise to provide us guidance. In Psalm 32:8 we read, "I will instruct you and teach you, in the way you should go; I will counsel you and watch over you."

An excellent verse for us to remember as Christians is Proverbs 3: 5-6. "Trust in the Lord with all your heart and lean not unto your own understanding; in all thy ways acknowledge Him, and He will make your path straight."

What is God's will for us?
1. Salvation- John 1: 12, 13 & Ephesians 1: 9, 10
2. Sanctification- 1 Thessalonians 4:3
3. Transformed Lives-Romans 12:2
4. To be thankful people- 1 Thessalonians 5: 18
5. To be good citizens- 1 Peter 2:5

God's specific will for Individuals! God doesn't really care if we eat steak or chicken, or whether we wear blue jeans or dress slacks. But when it comes to God's specific plan for our life work, we can be assured of His special guidance.

How can we know God's specific will? What are the pre-requisites?
1. Be a child of God. John 10:3- God promises to lead His children.
2. Obey what you already know. Mark Twain said, "It's not the parts of the Bible I don't understand that bothers me, but the parts I do understand."
3. Be willing to accept the will of God in unspecified areas of life before knowing what it is. Being able to say, "Not my will, but Thine be done!"

For most of us, this is where the real problem lies. Sometimes we want to say, "Lord show me your will so I can see how it fits in with my plans.".

How does God reveal His will?

1. Through Scripture. II Timothy 3: 14-15. Scripture deepens our consciousness of God. It brings us into contact with God. Teaches us God's principles and gives us examples for inspiration and warning.

2. Through Prayer- 1 John 5:14
For Wisdom- James 1: 5-6
Sense of Peace-Philippians 4: 6-7
Counsel of others- Proverbs 12:25
Circumstances- Doors open and close. Acts 16:6
Our own reasoning powers- 1 Corinthians 16: 5-9
Our own spiritual gifts-Romans 12: 3-8
When all of these factors- The Word of God, Conviction in Prayer, Circumstances and the Counsel of others are in line, it is usually a sign that God is leading and guiding us.

Illustration: A young sailor was learning the ropes from an experienced man of the sea. After spending the day on the water, night suddenly fell. The young sailor was concerned about returning to shore and finding the right way to go. The experienced sailor showed him three lights on the horizon and told him that they should sail toward the middle light. As they sailed for home, he noticed that the three lights started coming together. When they were in correct alignment with the docking space, the light converged into one light, and they knew they were home. When the parts of God's guidance come together, we know what God's will is.

God's will for your life is something far better than you can put together for yourself. I know, I proved it. He has taken me places I never dreamed I would go. He has given me the strength and courage to do things I never dreamed I could do.

People miss out on God's best when they are not willing to do His will.

Jehosophat- the Overcomer
II Chronicles 19: 1-10 & 20: 1-27

Although Jehoshaphat, through his affinity with Ahab fell into the mire, we do not find him wallowing in it. He must have been deeply ashamed on his return to Jerusalem, when Jehu, the son of the seer met him with a sharp rebuke, "Shouldn't you help the ungodly?" (vs 2) But this good this was found in him; he had already "prepared his heart to seek God." (vs 3). And God had already marked his repentance. As we look or recall chapter 18 which talks of his steps down to failure and shame, we note now his upward steps of faith to victory and joy. His work of faith is seen in the following ways:

1. Seeking the Restoration of Others.
a. Jehosophat went out again through the people and brought them back unto the Lord God. (19:4).
If they had been led away from the Lord through his evil example, now that he was restored in heart, he loses no time in using his influence for their good. The best work we can do for others is to bring them to Him, we bring them to the peace, power and plenty which only comes from God.

2. Justifying the ways of God.
"Now let the fear of the Lord be with you, for there is no iniquity with the Lord our God, nor respect of persons, or taking of gifts." (vs. 7)
These words were spoken to the judges of the land, The basis of their actions was to be the righteousness of God.

There is no false dealing with Him, no respect of persons, no taking of bribes. "He is the Lord, He is the Rock, His work is perfect, a God of truth and without iniquity, just and right is He. "(Deuteronomy 32:4)

3. Seeking God's help in the day of trouble.
After Jehosophat had decided to follow the Lord fully- the testing time came. The time was when he might have appealed to Ahab for help, having made a treaty with him, and 'sets himself to seek the Lord." (Vs 3) His example is followed by the whole nation for they "gathered themselves to ask help of the Lord."
Nations as well as individuals, must believe in the Lord to be saved, The man of faith knows no other God.

4. Answered Prayer
Jehosophat's faith in God is further evidenced by this sudden answer to his prayer. The spirit of the Lord came upon Jahaziel, as he stood in the midst of the congregation, with this message, "Be not afraid, nor dismayed by reason of this great multitudes, for the battle is not yours, but God's.
As soon as Jehosophat had put his trust in the Lord the battle became His. God takes over the responsibility of those who cast all their care upon Him.

5. Humble Acceptance
The revelation of God's saving power has always a head-bowing and heart-hallowing effect upon those to whom it comes in answer to faith and prayer.
The more deeply we drink of the river of God's grace, the more readily we bow and worship Him. He who

humbled Himself to the Cross for us has given the deathblow to our pride and self-sufficiency.
Jehosophat has proven for himself the truth of this, he speaks from experience. Faith in God must lead to faith in His prophets. The fruit of faith is not weakness and instability, but strength and prosperity, The Bible affords us many examples of those who have been strengthened and successful through their faith in God. "Faith laughs at impossibilities and says, "It shall be done." Jehosophat believed God and rejoiced in the hope of a glorious victory.

    Happy is the man who can sing praises to God for His word of promise and go on expecting miracles to happen. He shall not be disappointed. When they began to sing and praise the Lord, He set ambushes against the enemy, and they were smitten. (vs 22).
If the singers had been defeated, then might the enemies of the Bible rejoice; but the God of the Old Testament never fails to fulfill the expectations of all those who trust Him. This is the victory that overcomes the world, even our faith.

Working for Christ on the job!
Ephesians 6: 5-9

Most of us will work 160,000 hours during our lifetime. If we take few vacations and work after hours many will work about 200,000 hours. A housewife will work more than 290,000 hours. Work can either be drudgery or a delight.

As we look at Ephesians 6: 5-9 we see some good advice from the Apostle Paul for both laborers and employers. In Ephesians, Paul speaks to slaves (workers) and slave owners (employers). At the time in which he lived; more than 60 million slaves inhabited the Mediterranean area. Therefore, Paul spoke of the responsibility of slaves to their masters and masters to their slaves. But as he did, he dropped a bombshell into the world which eventually exploded into emancipation of people from slavery.

In this passage we see it in the light of what it means for us to work and to employ others. In place of the words "slaves" and "masters", I will use the words, employees and employers to help us better understand what is happening in the story. (Read that Scripture again).

Work can become a false god and the object of worship. We can spend our whole life trying to find meaning to our work. We can become workaholics, seeking to find our self-esteem in the approval of the people with whom we work.

How do you really feel about your work? Do you thank God for your job? Or are you waking up on Monday morning asking, "Is it Friday yet?"

I love my job as a Pastor, I Pastored several Churches for The Salvation Army over a span of 35 years and now in retirement, I continue ministry with my home Church, family and neighborhood in which I live. Pastoring, Shepherding, others are not easy. I had many sleepless nights throughout my career, but God gave me the strength to continue to push through. His grace is sufficient for all times, and all situations.

We don't usually think of enjoying our work as part of enjoying God. So, I ask, is it wrong to spend your life working at something that you do not enjoy? The apostle Paul has given us a powerful truth that cuts right to the core of how to glorify God in our work. He simply states that we are to treat people with whom we work as we would treat Christ.

1. What is your Vocation?

Vocation means calling. We are called first and foremost to belong to Christ, then to glorify Him and to enjoy Him in everything we do. In Christ no vocation is greater or more sacred than any other.

The Bible says to be in Christ is to be in the ministry. Life is not divided into the two categories of sacred and secular. Too often we think of work as drudgery or our workplace as a location where we can earn enough money to sustain us in life. We forget that everything in God's creation is sacred.

I like the way Paul talks about work in 1 Corinthians 10:31, "Whatever you do, do all to the glory of God." Can you say this about what you are doing? At work? Whatever your employment, be it typing, custodial, automotive, mechanic, medical profession, handyman, etc. it is sacred. Scripture tells us that all of life belongs to the Lord. Everything we do must be done to His glory. Have you ever considered your job as a ministry, as an exciting place to work for Christ?

2. What do you do for a living?

Could you or would you be able to explain your job if asked? If asked what I do for a living I respond, "Christ is my life, He is my living, He is who I work for every day of my life." The Apostle Paul did not tell the Philippians, "For me to live is to be a tentmaker." He said, "For me to live is Christ." He brought the dignity of Christ power to working with his hands as a tentmaker as much as he did to the preaching of the Gospel.

What do you do for a living? Christ is your living. Once you commit yourself to Him as the Lord of your life, then He will give you wisdom, strength, discernment, and power to work for Him, on and off the job.

The world is our calling as well. We are called to go into the world to be Christ to the lost, to bring hope, peace, joy. Things our world is so sorely lacking these days.

Reaching Out
Acts 8: 1-39

Every year Christian Life Magazine publishes a list of the 100 largest Sunday Schools in the United States. The Churches represented are from a variety of denominations; they use various kinds of curriculum material; they differ in several ways.

All of them have two things in common: They preach the Gospel of Christ and engage in evangelism. Up to now the early Christians were only taking the gospel into Jerusalem. So, an Evangelism Explosion began. It began with Stephn the first Martyr and continued to other parts of the world. One of the places it went was to Samaria.

1. Ministry in Samaria

Philip's preaching was accompanied by miracles. He healed the sick and cast out demons, out of those who were demon possessed. Philips ministry included not only something to listen to but something to look at. His miracles were like those of Jesus.

Some people think that to become a Christian involves giving up everything enjoyable and submitting to all sorts of unpleasant restraints. On the contrary.

Genuine Christianity brings joy. Salvation does not confine or restricts us, it frees us to go and do. It frees us from the prison of wrong habits and attitudes into "the glorious liberty of the children of God."

Satan tries to confuse people by counterfeiting the miracles of God. Today Satan is using this new world ideology to appeal to gullible people. The whole realm of the movements that we are seeing today are having a heyday. People are ready to believe anything-except the Bible.

Philip's message centered on the person and work of Jesus. People who had been giving attention to Simon were now giving attention to Philip and believing what he had to say. When Christians witness faithfully, enthusiastically and in the power of the Holy Spirit, people's heart will respond.

Simon listened with great interest to what Philip said. Perhaps he decided he would appear to become a Christian to gain control, for his own purposes.

Simon made a mistake that so many people make today. He though that he could buy the gift of laying hands on people so they could receive the Holy Ghost. Peter told him, the gift of God could not be bought. Peter's stern warning shows the seriousness of Simon's sin and the condition of his heart.

With the work done in Samaria the apostles returned to Jerusalem, and Philip was sent out on another mission, this time to one individual.

2. A Seeking Individual

An Ethiopian court Treasurer. He traveled to Jerusalem to worship. While traveling he was reading the Septuagint, the Greek version of the Old Testament. Philip ran over to a chariot and asked the Ethiopian if he understood what he was reading. He asked Philip to help him.

Philip gives us a valuable lesson in how God wants His people to share the Gospel with others. Most of us come into daily contact with people like this official. They're good people, respectable, but they're people who have no spiritual understanding, because they have not received Christ as Savior and so have not been given the Holy Spirit. Many of us, however, feel reluctant to talk to these people.

We all have heard hundreds of advertisements on a weekly basis that advertise their product, some give testimony of the effectiveness of the product they advertise. It works! People are buying into it. And so it is for Christianity. The best advertisement is a growing Christian, mature in their faith who's not afraid to tell others what Jesus Christ means to them and what Jesus has been doing in their life.

Apparently, Philip had mentioned baptism to the Ethiopian, for as the chariot came to a pool, the Ethiopian expressed his desire to be baptized. This is evidence that the man's heart had been ready for the Gospel. He wanted to know God but did not know how until Philip told him about salvation through faith in Jesus Christ.

After Philip baptized the Ethiopian, his work was done. The Ethiopian went on his way rejoicing. He preached the gospel in Ethiopia with great success and had many converts.

Philip preached his way from there to Caesarea which became his headquarters.

Philip's ministry should encourage all Christians who want to tell others about Jesus. Philip's ministry was a success because:

a. Everywhere he went, he preached Jesus Christ.
b. He did not allow racial, national, or cultural barriers to limit his ministry.

c.   He was sensitive to the Lord's leading and obedient to His direction.

d.   He used the Word of God in soul winning. To the extent that we are filled with the Spirit, God is able to use us in leading others to Jesus Christ as Savior and Lord.

Friends, salvation is free through Jesus. There is nothing we can do to earn it. We just repent of our sin, turn from our sinful ways, accept Jesus into our heart as Lord and Savior and you are on your way to a wonderful life of service through Him.

Delivered to Serve
Luke 1: 74 & 75

"Lord, keep alive my sense of wonder,
centering in the living Christ,
Oft placing me, His great throne under
To hold with Him a gracious tryst;
The old, old story ever new and ever proving itself true!

It is a great and cruel fallacy toward God and man to believe that we are saved merely to be satisfied. Such a debased thought is not worthy of the grace of God. The provision God made for us in Christ is to enable us to live before God, to love our fellowman, and labor for Christ and His cause.

1. The great deliverance

We are reminded here that this deliverance is:

<u>All of grace.</u> It is in reality, a Divine grant. It is because of His mercy that we are not consumed. When a board or society allows a grant to anyone, the idea of merit is often present, but with God's grants there can be no plea of merit, else grace is not grace.

2. <u>From the enemy, sin.</u>

Sin is one of the enemies out of whose hand we need deliverance. In giving us His Son, God has also given us a grant of freedom from sin. (Romans 6:18)

3. <u>From the enemy of self.</u>

If sin is not to be allowed to lord it over us, the self-seeking I must be put in a place of death. As long as the 'I' lives it will be the servant of sin.

4. <u>From the enemy Satan.</u> The great accuser, Satan, is always ready to bring some railing accusation against the Lord, against His Gospel, or against us as believers. (Ephesians 6:11). Put on the whole armor of God, that you may be able to stand.)

The Purpose of it! "He has delivered us that we might serve Him." We are saved to serve. (Romans 6:18) says, we have been freed from sin that we might become servants of God. It is good to be able to say, "thank God, I am saved," but it is better to be able to say, "Thank God, I am the bondslave of Jesus Christ. So that we might:

1. Serve Him. "Speak Lord for your servant hears." Serve Him, God first, not the Church, not a cause, not the good principle but the living Christ.

2. Serve Him without fear. We are living in a world that wants to silence Christians if they speak out against today's ideologies and movements that are contrary to Christian beliefs. If we love the Lord with all our hearts this will be the character of our service, for there is no fear in love; perfect love casts out fear. (I John 4:18)

3. Serve Him in Holiness. As saved ones, we are called with a holy calling. 2 Timothy 1:9). Called into the holy Priesthood, having been washed and clothed in holy things as we eat from His Holy Word.

4. Serve Him in Righteousness. Our new man is created after God in righteousness and true holiness.

(Ephesians 4:24). So the new man is expected to serve God in righteousness as well as holiness.

5. Serve Him diligently. Sweet is the service that is rendered in the consciousness of His presence and done as standing before Him. Serving Him is the remedy for the fear of man, and the secret of deliverance from dishonoring God by presenting eloquent prayers to great audiences.

6. Serve God all the days of our life. There is no discharge in this holy war. The Levite might retire after a limited number of years of service, but those delivered from sin and wrath by the agony and blood of Christ are to serve Him all the days of their life. In the days of bodily infirmity and weakness, when we can do nothing but look, may that look, be the look of blessed submission and holy trust.

The Channels Of Grace
1 Timothy 1:5

If we would value and love the Throne of Grace we must try to understand what it is that it provides for us. Scripture uses great words to reveal this grace to us. It speaks of "the riches of grace," the glory of grace, and the abundance of grace. Let these words sink deep into your heart as we point to them in God's Word.

I. The Divine Intention

In this text we are given the ultimate aim of divine grace in Jesus Christ, that we may be possessed by a spirit of charity. Charles Wesley writes: "Answer that gracious end in me for which Thy precious life was given," That end is clarity, stated here. It is surely a matter for deep reflection as to how far this is being accomplished in us.

God gave ten commandments to Moses on Sinai. Jesus gave us two. Here the divine intention is expressed in one word-Love. "Thou shalt love the Lord Thy God, with all you heart, with all your soul, with all your mind, and thou shalt love thy neighbor as thyself." By the spirit of Christ dwelling in us we are enabled to act kindly, speak charitably, think no evil and to be filled with goodwill toward all men.

There was a story told of a cobbler who was told to get ready, for soon the Lord was to visit his shop. He busied himself with preparations. But at various times during the day he was interrupted by people who wanted his help. There was a child with a broken toy, a woman with an urgent repair job, and some other needy callers. The cobbler turned none away, but patiently and kindly attended to them. At the close of day, he went to bed disappointed that the Lord had not come. Then he had a dream in which was shown to him that the Lord had visited him-when the child needed him, and when the woman requested his help. In receiving them with kindness and love, he received the Lord.

II. The Divine Implementation
Paul tells us how such a state can be realized. There are three factors.
    a.   A pure heart.
Believe in it. Conviction about this is one of the greatest necessities for Christ's people. Seek after it. Be ready for it. It is recorded of the Catherine Booth, The Mother of The Salvation Army that while busy about her household duties the Holy Spirit came to her and said that He would give her the blessing of a clean heart, for which she had long been seeking, there and then if she was willing to receive it. Kneeling in front of the kitchen fire she passed into that new and blessed experience, that "stern cleansing" of which we sing.
    "O forbid me not thy service, keep me yet in thy employ,
    Pass me through a sterner cleansing, if I may but give Thee joy! All my work is for the Master."
    b.   A good conscience.
If God's intention is to be implemented in us, we must keep a good conscience. This involves having a conscience about everything. Let the Holy Spirit enlighten and instruct us. If He tells us there is

something we should not read, or see or do, then we must be obedient. Keep a good conscience. Why expect the Holy Spirit to keep reminding us about things already made clear?

God guides in various ways, often through our own developed intelligence. "I prayed for advice, a man said, but nothing happened, the advice did not come, so I used my common sense." Could he not see that God was guiding him through his common sense?

c.   Faith unfeigned

Absolute honesty, absolute integrity, absolute sincerity. The most vital things relative to the life of God in the soul of man.

These three things mark us out as belonging to Christ. We have only to consider the effect in any community of people living in the spirit implied in this text to realize wherein lies the real power of the Christian faith.

A Life Sentence
Ephesians 3: 1-21

Paul's idea of service is as follows: "I will spend myself to the last ebb for you; you may give me praise or give me blame, it will make no difference."

So long as there is a human being who does not know Christ, I am His debtor to serve Him until I die.

The mainspring of our service is not love for men but love for Jesus Christ. If we are devoted to the cause of humanity, we shall soon be crushed and broken-hearted, for we shall often meet with more ingratitude from men then we would from a dog; but if our motive is love to God, no ingratitude can hinder us from serving our fellow men.

When we realize that Jesus Christ has served us to the end of our meanness, our selfishness, and sin, nothing that we meet with from others can exhaust our determination to serve men for His sake. If you are a follower of the Lord Jesus Christ, then you are committed to life. A life of service to Him and to others.

Does your commitment involve service?

Dietrich Bonhoeffer- Cost of Discipleship says: "Each follower of Christ must suffer. The first Christ-suffering which every man must experience is the call to abandon the attachments of this world and follow Him. (Jesus).

What is the importance placed on our commitment?

Is it important enough to surrender my life to? Will it satisfy me? Would God be pleased to bless me? Do people know that I am a Christian?

Charles Sheldon- Author of In His Steps- tells the story of a Pastor of a Methodist Church challenging his congregation to follow Jesus. Presenting the question to them, "what does it mean to follow Jesus?" Throughout the week a man, poor in health, depressed, lonely, went from house to house, business to business, trying to seek employment. He had doors slammed in his face. He knocked at this Methodist Ministers home seeking employment. The minister realizing that tomorrow was Sunday, and he had many interruptions already and must get a sermon done, hurriedly talked with the man, offered his sympathy and sent him on his way.

On Sunday this man found himself in this very illustrious Church, listened to the Pastor challenge his congregation to follow Jesus. The man interrupted, came forward and asked, "what does it mean to follow Jesus?" The man died a few days later, lonely, depressed, but he left a lasting impression on the congregation.

Does my commitment involve sacrifice and discipline?

Am I willing to deny pleasures in life in order to improve myself and become fit for my calling?

Is God glorified in my commitment?

As a Pastor, I often asked myself these questions. Not everyone can be a Pastor. But everyone can be a faithful servant of the Lord Jesus. Are we content with just being present in meetings, and occupying a place in the pew or band or songsters, or do we long to know more about God and His will for our life?

Carr/Sorley has penned the following prayer:

Lord, it would be simpler if your just let me be a Christian on my own terms. I prefer a respectable Christianity, a clean hands Christianity that doesn't step too far out of line. It is nice to be noble Lord, but I surely don't want to be conspicuous. If I am to help with the redemption of souls, let me redeem those with lesser sins- and leave the dregs for someone else.

Lord, I like being respectable. I like living in a nice house, in a good neighborhood, calling on nice people and having nice people call on me. It would be nice if all Your children would be respectable.

Father forgive, my soul is full of weeds. Jesus ate with sinners, ministered to the needs of the Samaritans. Respectable folk stood aghast at the things He said and did, at the inappropriate splendid things He said and did. Father, what I really want is to be splendid, to do the hard and splendid thing for You even if it makes me a misfit.

I wonder! Are you willing to be a misfit for Jesus. How is your commitment? Will it glorify God? Will it stand the test of time? Does it involve service? What importance do you place on it? Are you committed for life?

There is a chorus we sing in The Salvation Army that says:

If on my soul a trace of sin remaineth,
If on my hands a stain may yet be seen,
If one dark spot a weary soul retaineth
O wash me, Lord, that every part be clean;
For I would live that men may see Thyself in me,
I would in faith ascend Thy holy hill
And, with my thoughts in tune with Thy divinity,
Would learn how best to do Thy Holy will.

May God help each of us to know Him better, to Love Him supremely and be willing to be committed to Him for life.

Religious or Christian
Ephesians 4: 1-10

We are taught by Paul in this passage of Scripture that we have a vocation or a calling, and Jesus requires us to walk worthy of the calling we have received. That our every action, thought, word and deed, must be done unto the Lord.

We may say that we are a Christian, but do we really, walk it and talk it?

A poem has been written several years ago that says:

You're writing a Gospel a chapter each day, by the deeds you do and the words you say; people believe what you say, distorted or true, now tell me, what is the Gospel according to you?

Our vocation is a Christian calling; we are called Christians after Christ. When we, through His blood and forgiveness of sins has been adopted into His family, then we take on His name. And so as His child we must emulate Him. Do as He did, walk as He walked, talk as He talked, etc.

Our vocation is to live and die to Christ, to take Christ as our pattern, and work out in ourselves His image.

Seneca when in prison was deprived of all that remained of his possessions, they were confiscated; so, he bequeathed to his followers all that remained to him-the example of his life.

We have the example of Christ's life as our perfect pattern, and as the inheritance of every disciple of Christ; our work here is to study it and conform our lives to it.

Have you ever noticed a printer correcting a proof? He sets before him the copy, and goes over his work, and here's a wrong letter; he pulls it out and puts in the correct one. Here is a letter reversed, he extracts it, and places the correct letter in. And at last, he has conformed his type to the copy before him. You and I must deal with our lives that way. Set before you the copy, Jesus, and go over your actions, words, and thoughts and rectify them by the Copy which is perfect.

Too often, we want to put off getting saved until a convenient time, or too often we have the mistaken idea that because we go to Sunday School, Church, or even attend many of the meetings as we can, that we are a Christian, and that we are saved.

Being good does not save us, attending meetings does not save us. But sins forgiven and a personal relationship with the Lord Jesus will certainly guarantee us a place in God's Kingdom.

Several years ago, a young man was involved in an automobile accident and was placed on the critical list at the hospital. In the bloom of his youth and hours before pursuing many years of life, he was suddenly called to die. A preacher was summoned, and when the accident victim momentarily regained consciousness, he talked to him concerning his soul. "Oh, I did fully intend to be saved before the end of my lifetime. Trained in a Christian home and sensing that his moments were numbered, the man was frantic, for he was fully aware of the awful prospect of meeting death unprepared. Before he could be dealt with further, he once again lapsed into unconsciousness.

Two hours later his anguished spirit met its fateful appointment. Hebrews 9:27 says, "And as it is appointed unto man once to die, but after this is judgment.

A poem has been written which says:

The clock of life is wound but once, and no man has the power.
To tell just when the hands will stop, at late or early hour.
To lose one's wealth is sad indeed, to lose one's health is more,
To lose one's soul is such a loss as no man can restore.
The present only is our own; Live, love, toil with a will,
Place no faith in tomorrow for the clock may then be still.

You ask what is a Christian?

A Christian believes that God made the world and man in it. That man turned from God and that because of disobedience by Adam and Eve, sin came into the world.

A Christian believes that Jesus Christ was not another Philosopher, or Healer, but that He was in fact the true Son of God.

The Religious person believes that the world came about by evolution, the Big Bang theory and that man came from a monkey.

The Religious person believes that it is ok to do anything, whether that anything is good or bad.

I ask you right now to take a survey of yourself. Is your life the way it should be, are you a Christian or are you just going through the motions?

Perhaps the story of the young accident victim may be true of you. Will your dying hour be a convenient time for you should your body be racked with anguish, or your mind clouded by pain-relieving drugs? You may be called to meet your Maker without a moments warning. "God says, today-your deceived heart says, tomorrow."

The summer of opportunity may suddenly end. What an eternal tragedy if you must join the multitude of people who constantly cry, "We are not saved!"

The Apostle warns us, "Fight the good fight of faith, lay hold on eternal life; whereunto you are called." Called in baptism as soldiers enrolled, and called to what? Not just to fight as the end of our calling, but only a transient passage, an accident of our calling.

Are you a Christian or are you Religious? Have you been putting God off=for "better things?" God can and wants to meet your needs today. He can make you a genuine Christian. He can change your behavior and attitude. He can give you hope for the future.

A Spiritual Diet
1 Corinthians 9: 24-10: 1-13

We know that God loves us and provides and cares for His children. Why is it then that so many disobey Him and fall into sin and wrongdoing?

It is because they do not know what His will is. They are ignorant of His laws. They have not heard His Word. They are less to be blamed and more to be taught.

Sometimes it is because they make mistakes. Everybody makes mistakes at times. We may be mistaken in judgment or lacking in maturity. I have often said, and it bears repeating, "we sin everyday", yes, through our careless words, and actions toward God and one another. And because of that we have the freedom everyday to return to Him in humble repentance and ask for forgiveness. But be careful you do not continue to sin in the same way. A child who wants to help her father weed the garden may pull up the flowers with the weeds because they look alike.

We usually learn by our mistakes. We may be chagrined, we may feel very sorry, but we do not need to feel guilty. When our friends make mistakes, we should not condemn them but try to help them. As Paul put it: "Brothers, if someone is caught in a sin, you who are spiritual should restore them gently. But watch yourself, or you also may be tempted. Carry each other's burden's and in this way you will fulfill the law of Christ." (Galatians 6: 1,2) So therefore we need to acquire a:

1. Sensitivity to Sin:
    1. How subtle the devil is when he tempts us.
He puts questions in our minds, doubts our calling, our location, Ω
and even doubt our salvation.
Lord, make us sensitive to sin. Some of the temptations that Satan entices us with are: Idolatry-idols, Sexual immorality, lying, cheating, stealing, murdering, etc. Be careful you do not fall into Satan's trap. He is the great deceiver.

2. Sensitivity to the presence of God.
Perhaps if we were not as sensitive. To sin as we should be, then maybe we're not as sensitive to the presence of God that we should be.
How do we stay sensitive to His presence?
-Through communion and prayer. Do you look at prayer as a duty or delight?
-By Family devotions. It has been said, that a family who prays together, stays together.
- By obedience to His will. Our #1 priority will be to win souls for Him.
- Be aware of Him in all you do. As you walk around your neighborhood, in stores, at work, everywhere know that God is there. He is present.
- Exercise faith. He's all He says He is and we can trust Him in all things.

When people choose to do wrong, they sin, for they know that they are disobedient to God. This may be because they want to do their own thing. Ego gets in the way. Sometimes a person sins because it is the easiest way out, until they're caught.

Adam and Eve sinned because of disobedience. It is well then to realize that, on a given occasion in history, two real people, Adam and Eve, were tempted by a very real devil, Satan, and disobeyed a very real God.

Do you have a sensitivity to sin, or do you give much thought to it?

Has sin crept into your life? Has it been allowed to remain or have you committed it to the Lord, seeking His forgiveness.

Do you know God's perfect will for your life? Are you obeying that will or running from it?

Not I, but Christ
Galatians 2:20

What a difference it would make in our lives, if we could take time every morning to be filled with the though; Christ in me! Through the power of God all we who believe were crucified with Christ, raised again with Him. Through faith in God's Word the Christian accepts it, and the Holy Spirit will lead us into all truth.

Think of these two personalities:
"I" and "Christ". There is a mystery in each of them.
"I". The mystery of evil an instrument of the devil.
"Christ" The mystery of Godliness, servant of God.

Each is the medium through which another great personality works. This unregenerate "I" in its ignorance, selfishness, pride, unbelief, is a fit subject for the Prince of Darkness-Satan.

The Heaven anointed Christ in His unselfish devotion to the will of God, is perfectly fitted for the accomplishments of God's purposes.

William Law said, "Self is the root branches, the tree of all the evils of our fallen race." This should be modified by saying; the unsurrenered self is the root of all the evils of our fallen self.

Think of this relationship with one to another. What is there in common between this "I" and the "Christ" between the servant of Satan and the servant of God? What communion has light with darkness? Each is animated and controlled by a different and opposing spirit. The principles of the flesh and the Spirit are contrary to one another.

That which is born of the flesh is flesh, and that which is born of the Spirit is Spirit. And belongs to the Kingdom of God. Corruption cannot inherit incorruption. Self is carnal. Christ is Spiritual. "To be carnally minded is death to the Spiritual things of life. (Romans 8:6). This "I" the natural man, receives not the things of the Spirit of God, and so can have no fellowship with Christ.

God is a jealous God! He wants to be #1 in your life.

Think of the meaning of this new relationship, "Not I, but Christ." These words imply a putting off of the old man and putting on of Christ. "I" has surrendered and given place to the life of Christ. "It's no longer I that lives but Christ that lives in me."

Is He first in your life? Is He Lord over your life?

The Holy Spirit is at work in our life!
John 16: 1-15

In this passage of Scripture, the writer is speaking about our lack of sensitivity to the Holy Spirit of God in the common places of our daily living.

The mind of mortal man cannot comprehend the clash of God and Satan in the tense, harsh atmosphere of the humble, common upper room where Jesus celebrates the Feast of the Passover with His intimate fellowship of Disciples. The quiet setting is a refuge from the hatred of the enemy, but Heaven and Hell share the common table.

Satan had contended for and won the heart of Judas, the betrayer. He had seeded rejection in the mind and heart of Peter, who had just, with an oath, denied his discipleship and his relationship with Christ. The evil one has spread his shadowy net of fear over the minds of the disciples and soon they too will flee into the darkness and leave Him alone in the clutches of His tormenters and executioners.

But He who is the Spirit of love and whose heart is broken for their sakes, is speaking of One who will restore that which is broken, who will heal that which is wounded, and give life to that which is dead. Jesus speaks with simplicity of the coming Holy Spirit who will possess them, forgive them, empower them and lead the into the intimate fellowship of His presence.

The Two Sons
Matthew 21: 28-32

This message begins with Christ's question, "what do you think?" and is eminently fitted to make us think. Some parish for want of thought and many more fo wrong thinking. The priests and elders had been asking Him, "By what authority do you do these things?"

Christ answers the question by holding up this parable as a mirror before their eyes that they might be convinced of their sins. The way to understand the authority of Christ is to discover our real state before Him. Those who pride themselves in their own supposed goodness will always remain in ignorance of Christ's authority and saving power.

What the Father Commanded. (vs. 28)

"Son go, work today in my vineyard." The Father's vineyard needs workers there is much to be done; and who should be more interested in helping than the sons since they will most likely inherit the land.

Let's look at the grounds of the Father's claim. (vs 28).

There are plenty of people that could be hired to do the work, but love ought to constrain the son. How often have you asked your child to clean their room, mow the lawn, etc. and the child has agreed to do so for a price.

If we are the sons and daughters of God, surely our Father has the first claim upon our time, our strength and our substance. Our Father may hire strangers to do the work, but as His children we are commanded to work, at no cost.

What grief it must be to our God to see so much work to be done, and so many of His children idle! Work is pleasing to the father, good for the vineyard and profitable for the Son. The idle soul will suffer hunger. (Proverbs 19:15) Our Father has a multitude of talkative children who talk about work, but there are few workers.

In the case of the first son there was a decided refusal. (vs. 29) "I will not." This language reveals the spirit of selfish indifference to the father's desire. In plain words, he says, "I have something else of my own to do, and I don't have time to work in your vineyard." What cares the selfish Christian for the perishing millions or the grieving heart of the Father, if their own plans and purposes can only be attended to. This kind of language portrays a heart in open rebellion. "I will not>" I can just picture the son not only saying those words but like a child, stomping his feet as he says them. A life possessed to the father's will and out of sympathy with the Father's purpose.

The second son answers with a ready consent. (vs. 30) "I will go sir."

Judging from his talk he has a great reverence for his father and great earnestness to work. This kind of instant decision and prompt reply to the father's command should be copied by everyone of us who call ourselves children of God.

What the sons did in response to the request are different. There is a vast difference between a man's profession and his actions. The question is: "Which of these sons did the will of the father? Not which of them talked the best or made the loudest profession. By their deeds are they justified or condemned. His Word is fulfilled in our doing, not our thinking about it.

The one son repented and obeyed. Repentance always precedes the doing of the will of God. Thos who go willingly into the Father's vineyard of Service will find grace sufficient and a holy joy in pleasing Him.

The other son promised and failed. He said, "I'll go!" and He did not. All who do not go at God's bidding into the field of service for Him are disobedient and rebellious children no matter how nice they may talk about the Lord's work. "Talking about ministry opportunities, ministers, churches, is not working for God any more than warming our hands by the fire is." Not everyone that says, "Lord, Lord will enter into the kingdom, but he who does the will of the Father. "Whatsoever He says to you, do it." (John 2:5)

Where do we go from here?
Psalm 32: 1-9

"I will instruct thee and teach thee in the way you shall go."

The way is provided for us-Jesus is the Way.

John Wayne in the "Quiet Man" was asking directions for the Way to Innespree. The Train Conductor, Engineer and Ticket Collector all argued about which way it was. Barry Fitzgerald came along-picked up John Wayne's bags and took him to Innespree- He became the way.

Jesus is the Way- He doesn't point it out to us-He lifts our burden and goes with us. Just as John Wayne had to sit on the back of the horse and buggy to follow Barry Fitzgerald-so we have to put ourselves in the hands of Jesus and follow where He leads.

God is interested in us individually. There is no one like you. God broke the mold when He made you. We are all unique and each has a contribution to make.

There is life in Christ. He has a divine will for all of us to know.

"I will guide Thee with mine eyes" Vs. 8.

The Lord's prayer says, "Thy will be done in Earth as in Heaven."

What is the will of God in Heaven? That His Son Jesus Christ be Lord.

When God gives us this new life it entails responsibilities-

Toward family- Praying for our family will produce better people.

In the Church-Friendliness toward strangers. Local leadership is much needed and must be an example to the young people.

The sense of sacredness will permeate all we do when we really, "leave all" to follow Him.

He gives power to rise above difficulties and temptations. These are not always removed, but He gives strength and patience to meet them and to overcome.

Colonel Bramwell Tripp, Retired Pastor The Salvation Army, in his book, "To The Point" states this. "Men ought always to pray" because power is needed. The only way we can get God's help is to ask for it. Through prayer we make vital connection with the eternal and wonder-working power. Energy that appears inaccessible is activated and made available by prayer."

Isaiah 40:32-"They that wait upon the Lord will renew their strength; they will mount up with wings like eagles. They shall run and not be weary. They shall walk and not faint."

To "rise up" is to strive toward spiritual maturity in Christ through every means at our disposal. Matthew's life was lived in new company, for he not only left all to follow Christ, but it brought him into a Supreme Association.

We like to be in the company of people we admire, so that to "follow Christ" means that we will, enjoy His company. Not only for a brief time, in the morning or evening, nor when in special need, but practicing His presence all day long.

We must seek to develop a character like His and say to others, "follow me" I know the way.

Christ calls us to be disciples! We are told in John 8:31, "Then are you my disciples indeed". Christ calls us to be His Disciples and to take up our cross and follow Him. We are called to be soul-winners.

When in I hope will help you as it has me. "When we get to heaven the Lord will give us a stone in our crown representing every soul that we won into His Kingdom." How many that we receive, will be life's greatest reward. Oh to see the joy on God's face! And for us to know that we did it all because of love that we have for His Son, Jesus Christ who died for us, that we might have everlasting life in Heaven. That will be life's greatest, most thrilling reward for us who call ourselves "Christian."

The way we walk, the way we live, our example can be used to win somebody to Christ. II Corinthians 5:20 tells us. "Now then we are ambassadors for Christ. We are living examples of the Christ, who saved us and called us to be soul-winners. Is the Holy Spirit speaking to you about this challenge? If so, respond to His voice. You will never be the same.

The Great Commission-Go and Preach
Mark 16: 15-20

A well known authority on missions has said, "Christianity is the only religion that is Missionary."

This call has come down through all ages beckoning weary souls to come and rest.

1. The Need: This is summed up in one word, "World!" Go into all the world. Many believe the world means some foreign country, or remote place. But the world as well means your neighborhood, friends, family. All who are outside of the will of God. We are called to Rescue the Perishing!
Our sinful self is the devil's nursery, where every evil in the world is germinated, transplanted by actual deeds, into this world, the power of Christ must come. We must get out of the way and allow God to have His way.
We sing a chorus in our Church that says:
It's no longer I that liveth, but Christ that liveth in me.(Repeat)
He lives, He lives, Jesus is alive in me.
It's no longer I that liveth, But Christ that liveth in me.

2. The Provision: "Go and Preach the Gospel to every nation for the Gospel contains good tidings of great joy to all people".
We have been purchased by the Blood of the Lamb (Jesus) . He was sinless but took our sins upon Himself to the cross and died that we might live eternally with Him. When I think of such love I become overwhelmed

to think that someone would love me enough to die for me.
He paid a debt He did not owe,
I owed a debt I could not pay'
I needed someone to wash my sins away.
And now I sing a brand new song,
Amazing Grace the whole day long,
Christ Jesus paid a debt that I could never pay.
If He had not died for us, we would have no hope. He paid that debt with His life on the Cross for you and me.

3. The Commission-"Go into all the world," A message, simple, clear, and definite. As the Father sent Me, so send I you! (John 17:18)
The promise of that commissioning is- "Lo I am with you always!" His presence is the pledge of continual fellowship. If His presence is not realized or enjoyed, it is not that His promise has failed, but that self-or sin has grieved the Holy Spirit Who makes His presence a reality and power.
There will be continual victory-There can be no victory over the enemies of God if His presence is not with us.
There is the fulfillment- They went forth and preached everywhere, the Lord working with them. (Verse 20). They were obedient, they went forth, like Abraham leaning on God's Word.
They were successful. The Lord working with them and confirming the Word. If the Lord is not working with us, our labor is in vain. The Lord will work with us if we are wholly yielded to doing His will. Preaching

to everyone we come in contact with the message of the good news of the Gospel.

Dare To Be Different
Ephesians 4:17-32

We live in a scary world. We are being asked to conform to one ideology after another. To deny our faith, and surrender control, more or less to government.

We must dare to be different. We must not only know who we are, but Whose we are.

We all have traits of being daring, whether good or bad. Children and young adults will often dare each other to do some dramatic feat.

No Christian dares another Christian to give up their profession. To accept a dare will often lead to sin. Christ tells us we must:

1. Dare to be Soldiers of Jesus Christ.

Dare to stand firm in your belief. Other people need to know we are Christians, by the way we live, by our walk, and by our talk.

We must uphold the Christian standards. The Christian standards are high. They must be kept high and should never be lowered for any reason or anyone. The world must see in everything we do that we are Christians.

Elton Trueblood-:"

Company of the Committed" says: " A person cannot be a Christian and avoid being a Soul-Winner. Soul Winning is not a professional job of a few gifted or trained people, but the unrelenting responsibility of every person who belongs to the family of God."

2. Dare to Be Different

In the world in which we live, that is scary. People don't want to hear anything about Christianity, Christians are being silenced. It takes a brave Christian to be obedient to God's will, though it may mean dying for His sake.

As an Officer (Pastor) in The Salvation Army, requires obedience to God's Spirit. And complete surrender to His will.

I would not have made it over 50 years in ministry if I failed to realize very early in my ministry that Jesus Christ had to be the head of my life. That He required from me my total allegiance to Him and His will for my life.

Ministry has never been about me. It has been about Jesus who is Lord of my life, and His amazing Grace that has been more than sufficient for me.

In Daniel 6: 1-28, King Darius wrote a decree that stated, "anyone who prays to any god or human being during the next thirty days, except to you, Your Master, shall be thrown into the lions den." Daniel, hearing about the decree went home to his upstairs room where the windows opened toward Jerusalem. Three times a day he would pray to his God. Then a group of men who saw him praying went to the King and asked. "Did you not publish a decree during the next thirty days anyone who prays to another god shall be thrown in the den of lions? The King confirmed the decree and the group of men said that Daniel was praying to his God, and she should be thrown in the den of lions! So, the King ordered that Daniel be thrown into the den of lions. But because of Daniel's great faith in the God

whom he served, found him innocent, and God shut the mouths of the lions and Daniel was not hurt.
God is faithful! He loves His own with an everlasting love.

3. Dare to be Different.
Don't be satisfied with what you are. Dare to be Different. Dare to be a Daniel.
There is a song we sing in the Church that says:
Dare to be a Daniel, Dare to stand alone
Dare to have a purpose firm and dare to make it known.
Standing by a purpose true, heeding God's command
Honor them the faithful few all hail to Daniel's band.
Many mighty men are lost daring not to stand.
Who for God had been a host by joining Daniel's band.
Many giants great and tall stalking through the land
Headlong to the earth would fall if met by Daniel's band.
Hold the Gospel banner high on to Victory grand,
Satan and his hosts defy and shout for Daniel's band.
Dare to be a Daniel, dare to stand alone,
Dare to have a purpose firm and dare to make it known.
    Philip P. Bliss 1873

 Written over 150 years ago the message is still the same.
 Temptation will come. It comes to all of us, but we are, more than Conqueror through Him!"
 It has been said that what has been attributed as ferocity to the tiger is due to incredible audacity and courage. It simply sees no danger, knows no fear, abandons no object of attack.

Are these the elements of Christian courage?

If we are filled with a deep sense of God's presence and power, and of our own privileges and responsibilities, would this not blind us to many of the things that disturb and terrify, and inspire to many an act and work which we now dread.

We must display a Christlike attitude always.

We must dare to be different.

Thomas-Delivered from Doubt
John 20: 19-29

One who is involved near the end of our Lord's life. This passage leads us to accept the title given to this character "Doubting Thomas."

Mary was another doubter when in the verses prior to these, when she found the rock rolled away, she felt someone had stolen His body. She did not believe Him to be resurrected.

In none of the lives of the disciples do we see anyone expecting a resurrected Lord. They all doubted. Well then why do we just single out Thomas as the doubter, maybe because he was so bold about expressing his doubt.

Jeremiah, what battles he went through and what doubts he had. He was sure God had forsaken him. "Will you be to me like a deceitful brook, God?" You're there, but you are not there.

Jeremiah was not a sinner, he was a child of God, a servant of the Lord. Thomas was not a sinner; he just couldn't believe. How do you therapeutically minister to a person going through doubt and dark nights? If handled improperly a doubt has the potential to become spiritual suicide. If handled properly it can become a cornerstone of faith. Thomas is dealing with deceit. Discouragement, depression and is a candidate of the Elijah Syndrome-It is better that I'm dead.

The other disciples sit him down and said, "guess what Thomas, Jesus is alive." Thomas doesn't share in the excitement because he needs proof. He needs more personal encounters with the Lord. There are a few things commendable about Thomas:

1. His Honesty-he refused to say he believed when he really didn't. He didn't fake it. We're all good fakers, we know what to say, when to say it, and how to say it to be accepted in a group.

A young person buys a $40.00 pair of faded jeans, cuts holes in them, just to be accepted.

Thomas didn't care. Most of us would rather conform than be honest. Conformity is a deadly sin. How many have sacrificed honesty for acceptance? Thomas was willing to share where he was in his life.

2. He wanted to find out for himself the truth.
He didn't want to accept what someone else said about it. He was in essence saying, "I need to find out for myself", I can't ride on your coat tail!

John 4: 17 speaks about the Woman at the Well. She was a Samaritan. She went to the well to get water as she did daily and had an encounter with Jesus. He told her all about what she had done in her life. After her encounter, she went back and shared with those in her village about this man, who loved her with no strings attached, unconditionally, some believed. A while later, Jesus Himself came in person and they believed. What she shared was confirmed.

3. When Thomas encountered the One who was the Truth, he embraced it totally and completely. Nothing stood in the way. Thomas could then honestly say, "My Lord, and my God!"

Thomas has something to say to us about honesty. How do we deal with life and those around us? Do we speak honestly, deal honestly with all people? Do we put on a front and make people think we are what we really aren't? People, we are only fooling ourselves. God knows all about us, we can't put on a front with Him.

A Life of Obedience
Philippians 2: 12-18

A visitor to South India dropped in at a Men's Fellowship where 20 national Christian's were meeting for prayer and Bible Study. Besides their group devotions the men went regularly to nearby towns and villages to share the Gospel with their Hindu countrymen.

The guest asked, "As you engage on your evangelistic work, what objection to the Gospel do you meet most often?

The most experienced man in the room replied. "The obstacle is the inconsistent lives of Christians." Others in the group nodded their assent. They had met the same difficulty. In what ways are we as Christians, "walking testimonials" to the validity of the Christian faith?

Following his great discourse in verses 5-11, Paul now seeks to immediately apply what he has taught. He is answering the questions, "so what?"

As we look at verse 12 we see that a second "Therefore appears." The first appeared in verse 9. This provides Paul with the leverage to launch into a discussion of appropriate action. Merrill Tenney has observed that Philippi, was founded by Philip, the father of Alexander the Great. It was a center for mining gold and silver. How appropriate, then, that Paul used a contemporary expression for the mining process. The writer Strabo used it with reference to silver mines in Spain. He indicated that the one than "be worked out." In other words, they should bring to the surface what was buried under the earth.

God told us in the Bible to do something and then we talk about "waiting on Him," We are simply talking when we should be doing. We are the ones who must "work out" our salvation.

In Verse 13 it says we must work. But as we work, "it is God who works" within us. Paul illustrates this Biblical combination in Colossians 1:29. Over our rightly motivated work we may imagine the words painted, "God at Work". Imagine the privilege as a believer to know that Almighty God is working in me: graciously helping me not only to do good, but also to want to do good.

In verse 14 there is an emphasize on the person's doing. It is not just what is done but how it is done: "without complaining or arguing." This implies not only a limit on outward behavior but also an exhortation to deal with the attitude producing such behavior: a spirit of jealousy or envy, unrealistic expectations, unfair comparisons.

Now the goal of our actions is presented in verse 15. To become "blameless and pure", child of God without fault in the context of a crooked and depraved generation. Here Paul uses a vivid comparison. We are like stars in the universe, who shine out for all to see and admire.

We are born to grow, but growth is not inevitable or automatic. There are laws that regulate growth. For example: If you want to grow physically, you must eat regularly; you must exercise. No one questions these laws; we accept them without argument. But when it comes to spiritual growth, we often seem to feel that it should occur automatically. It seems that many Christians have a hard time accepting one of the basic principles of spiritual growth: Growth requires effort. Try evaluating your own life in terms of spiritual growth.

I want to provide you with a list of 5 areas providing the context for Christian growth, with some practical ways of applying them in your daily life.

1. We need to have goals. Goals for Bible Study and Prayer: I am an early riser. I get up at 4:30 a.m., I fix a cup of coffee then I meet with God. I have my Bible open to the next chapter that I want to read, a notepad beside me to take notes, and I pray. It must be intentional. You can't meet with God once weekly; He wants to meet with you every day.

2. We must set goals in our daily life as we walk this earth. We need to pray for a new attitude and make new commitments.

3. We must develop the habit of rejoicing even in bad circumstances, offering thankful prayers.

4. We need to practice the truth. Tell the truth always everywhere.

5. We must develop a life of purity. Pure thoughts, language, and pure in our daily habits.

In verse 16 Paul exhorts us to not only grow, but also to hold fast to the Gospel they have come to understand. Paul's boasting "on the day of Christ" will be due to the Philippians own actions born out of right attitudes. This "boasting" will not be pride, but rather an indication of his desire to keep working in futility: "that I did not run or labor for nothing." 1 Thessalonians 2: 19-20.

Paul in verse 17 implies that it is not he who is offering, but rather God who is offering Paul's involvement and commitment in service as a sacrifice. It is a sacrifice upon sacrifice of the Philippians. So then, even if Paul is a sacrifice upon a sacrifice, he "congratulates" the Philippians on their good work. Such dependence on God, along with selfless commitment to fellow believers, is a model for our own behavior.

In verse 18, Paul says that it is the will of God that Christians should be much in rejoicing. Notice that they rejoice both in work they are doing and accomplishing and with Paul in the results of their labor rejoices with them. Another leadership quality of Paul's was his willingness to share his joys with those he led.

Are you living a life of obedience?

All You Could Hope For
Matthew 25: 14-30

Young people today feel they've got it all together. They can express their views and they expect to be heard. They're explorers, exploring every new and different thing that comes their way, and still, they're unhappy, and life for them seems uncertain. Teenagers of today, BEWARE! About 150 years ago young people found their place in society, they were heard, life had meaning.

Flora Larrson author of "MY Best Men Are Women" relates. Numerous stories of young people who expressed their views, fought for a cause and were heard.

Lt. Eliza Shirley was actively engaged in full-time service at the age of 16. When she turned 17 years old, she was put in charge of a Salvation Army Center in Wales, there she experienced hundreds of people coming to the Lord through her faithful ministry to them. There was an occasion when two teenagers were found ministering to a congregation that they gathered from the streets.

Countless numbers of young people have led the march against sin, they've taken their stand for Christ, and they have been heard.

We are each important and we each one have a job to do.

There's a story of a man who left all to find the largest diamond in the world-finally he returned home after many months of searching. While doing his daily work of gardening he came upon the largest diamond right there, in his own yard.

It sounds a little far-fetched, but don't we go out of our area, families, towns, seeking importance when all the time we've had it. So many things we search for, to be like someone great, and someone we admire, and all too often we fail to realize that who we are is not as important as Whose we are. Beloved you are Royalty. You are a child of the King of King. God loves you just the way you are and wants to save you and bring you into His family.

We can't get so hung up on trying to achieve prestige that we lose sight of the reason for which we've been called, and that is to glorify God and win men and women, boys and girls to Him. There is no higher calling.

We must consider this, that we as a beautiful diamond must start from:

1. Raw Material

A Diamond has no real form, it is a rock, no brilliancy., There is no hope in the diamond, no promise for the future unless worked with.

A story is told in Matthew 25 of the Parable of the Talents, and what each man did with the talents they received. The first two men, out their talents to good use and therefore increased the number of talents that they possessed, The third man however hid his talent, and the talent became worthless.

We must not hide our God given gifts however great or small they might be.

To become a perfect diamond, it takes skilled and loving hands, it takes the:

2. Master's Touch

There must first be a cutting away of unnecessary parts, parts that hinder. There must be as we sing in the Church that: breaking, melting, molding and mending. The quality of cut will increase the value and beauty.

Myra Brooks Welch described it so well in her poem entitled: The Touch of the Master's Hand.

Twas battered and scarred, and the auctioneer thought it scarcely worth his while to waste much time on the old violin but held it up with a smile.

"What is my bid, good folks", he cried, "Who'll start the bidding for me"?

A dollar, a dollar and who'll make it two, Two dollars and who'll make it three?

Going for three but no, from the room, far back, a gray hair man' came forward and picked up the bow; then wiping the dust from the old violin.

And tightening the loose strings, he played a melody pure and sweet as a caroling angel sings.

The music ceased, and the auctioneer, with a voice that was quiet and low,

"What is my bid fo this old violin and he held it up with the bow.

A thousand dollars, and who'll make it two?" "Two thousand and who'll make it three thousand twice and going and gone said he."

And many a man with life out of tune and battered and scarred with sin.

Is auctioned cheap to the thoughtless crowd, much like this old violin.

A mess of pottage, a glass of wine, a game and he travels on. He is going, once, going twice and almost gone.

But the Master (Jesus) comes, and the foolish crowd never can quite understand.

The worth of a soul and the change that is made, by the touch of the Master's hand.

We need to let our light shine that others may see Christ in us. It is not about us. So many walk this world on an ego trip. Turn your eyes upon Jesus, take them off of worldly things. He's got you!

We've come a long way in over 2000 years. We've been privileged to have freedom of worship, and still there are many people who live in darkness, right here in our own country.

Diamonds come in many sizes and shapes, but each individual one given in love is of equal importance. We spend time seeking to be a HOPE DIAMIND and forget we are valuable and important in the Kingdom of God. There are no insignificants with Him.

You are more valuable than you realize if Christ dwells within you. May God help you and me to be durable, strong, and beautiful for Him.